The Best Ever Book of Table Tennis Jokes

*Lots and Lots of Jokes
Specially Repurposed for You-Know-Who*

Other books by Mark Young

The West Australian Joke Book
How To Promote Your Business
Dr. Young's Guide to Demotivating Employees
Guide To Selling Your Home

And about 600 other books titled:

The Best Ever Book of ...... Jokes

To find out more, check out our websites at:

www.dolyttle.com, www.thebesteverbook.com

or visit

www.amazon.com

THE BEST EVER BOOK OF TABLE TENNIS JOKES

*Lots and Lots of Jokes
Specially Repurposed for You-Know-Who*

Dolyttle & Seamore
New York, New York

The Best Ever Book of Jokes: Lots and Lots of Jokes Specially Repurposed for You-Know-Who

Dolyttle & Seamore
New York, New York

© Copyright 2012. All rights reserved. No part of this book may be reproduced or transmitted in any form or by any means, electronic or mechanical, including photocopying, recording or by any information storage and retrieval system, without the written permission of the publisher.

Limit of Liability/Disclaimer of Warranty: While the publisher and author have used their best efforts not to offend while preparing this book, some people will no doubt be offended. As a result, no representations or warranties are made or inferred with respect to the accuracy or completeness of this book, or the truth of any of the statements. It comes with no warranties, implied or otherwise, of merchantability or fitness for a particular purpose. We do not guarantee that any of the people mentioned in this book are real, and if they are real, no similarity is intended or inferred. Should the people in this book actually exist, this book makes no character judgement about them or their friends, families, relatives and other people they may know now, in the future or in the past. Be warned. The jokes in this book may not suit your needs or tastes. If you are concerned about being offended, and have already paid for this book, put it down now and take steps to destroy it, as neither the publisher or author shall be liable for any damages or losses made to any groups of people or individuals who may or may not be mentioned in this book. This includes, but is not limited to special, incidental, consequential or other damages. YOU HAVE BEEN WARNED.

Dolyttle & Seamore
198 Garth Road Suite 2DD
Scarsdale, NY 10583

Publisher's Cataloging-in-Publication Data

The Best Ever Book of Jokes: Lots and Lots of Jokes Specially Repurposed for You-Know-Who.

p. cm.
ISBN-13:9781478120100
ISBN-10:147812010X

10 9 8 7 6 5 4 3 2 1

To All Those People
Who Think They Have a Sense of Humor —But Don't

Introduction

In my world, nothing is original. While I may be the only person who believes this, it's true. I have heard almost every joke in this book at least a hundred times—the only difference is the victim—a different ethnic, racial or religious group.

I grew up in Australia where the victim was Irish. In other states and countries the victim is often Jewish, Blond, Italian, Libyan, Catholic, Mexican, Polish, Australian, Norwegian, Essex Girl, Newfie, Mother-in-Law, etc.

Just because the person being picked on varies from country to country, it doesn't mean they're a hated minority. I would argue that it means that they're loved (after all, almost everybody wants to be the center of attention). In most cases, the goal is not humiliation, because the jokes being told are not nasty—they're funny—or at least they're supposed to be.

With that said, sit down, put on your happy face and prepare to be transported back to a time when you were young and innocent, and your friends tried to put a smile on your face.

And, if you're offended, sorry, no offence is intended. Just remember that perception is everything, and the way you perceive these jokes says a lot about you.

Mark Young

Why do people take an instant dislike to Table Tennis Players?

To save time later.

Two Table Tennis Players were helping a friend open a new store, and decided to take a break. Since the shop wasn't due to open for a few days, the shelves were not fully set up.

One Table Tennis Player said to the other: "I bet some old fogey will walk by, put his or her face to the window, and ask what we're selling."

No sooner were the words out of his mouth, when an old woman peeked through the window and cheerfully asked: "What are you selling?"

"We're selling assholes," replied one of the Table Tennis Players sarcastically.

Without skipping a beat, the lovely old lady said: "You must be doing well. You've only got two left."

What do you call a Table Tennis Player who practices birth control?

A humanitarian.

Why do Table Tennis Players make great astronauts?

They took up space in school.

Two Table Tennis Players were riding their bikes across a university campus when one said: "Where did you get such a great bike?"

The second Table Tennis Player said: "I was walking across town yesterday, minding my own business, when a beautiful woman rode up on this bike, threw it to the ground, took off all her clothes and said: "Take what you want."

The first Table Tennis Player nodded approvingly and said: "Good choice; the clothes probably wouldn't have fit you anyway."

There was a Table Tennis Player who was late for work during the power failure because he got stuck on the escalator.

Two Table Tennis Players in a kayak were chilly, so they lit a fire in the craft. It sank, proving once again that you can't have your kayak and heat it too.

A Table Tennis Player was staying with a friend and asked if there was anything he could do to help out.

"Sure," said the friend. "I'd really appreciate it if you could pick up a carton of milk when you're out. If they have eggs, get six."

A couple of hours later the Table Tennis Player returned with six cartons of milk.

"Why did you buy six cartons of milk?," asked the friend.

"They had eggs," replied the Table Tennis Player.

Why did the Table Tennis Player cut a hole in the carpet?

To see a floor show.

Did you hear about the Table Tennis Player who went to a mind reader?

There was no charge.

Why don't Table Tennis Players eat pickles?

They can't get their head in the jar.

A Table Tennis Player met a fairy who said she would grant her
one wish.

"I want to live forever," said the Table Tennis Player.

"Sorry," said the fairy. "I can't grant wishes like that!"

"Fine," said the Table Tennis Player. "I want to live until Congress gets its heads out of its ass!"

"Crafty bastard," said the fairy.

A Table Tennis Player with one ear want into a bar.

"Do you want a beer?," asked the bartender.

The Table Tennis Player: "I've got one ear."

Four workers were on the top floor of a high-rise building project when Steve fell off the roof and died instantly.

After the body was taken away by the ambulance, they held a meeting to decide who would tell Steve's wife that he was killed in a horrible accident.

Finally, one of the workers said: "I used to be a Table Tennis Player, so I'm pretty good at delivering bad news, I'll do it."

Two hours later, he came back carrying a case of beer.

"Where did you get the beer?," asked one of the workers.

"Steve's wife gave it to me," he said.

The worker replies: "That's unbelievable, you told the lady her husband was dead and she gave you the beer?"

"Well not exactly," said the Table Tennis Player. "When Steve's wife answered the door, I said to her: 'You must be Steve's widow.'"

She said: "No, I'm not a widow."

And I said: "I'll bet you a case of beer you are."

How did the Table Tennis Player die ice fishing?

She was run over by the Zamboni machine.

Hear about the Table Tennis Player who broke both legs ironing the curtains?

She fell out the window.

An evil genie captured a Table Tennis Player and her two friends and banished them to the desert for a week. The genie allowed each person to bring one thing.

The first friend brought a canteen so he wouldn't die of thirst.

The second friend brought an umbrella to keep the sun off.

The Table Tennis Player brought a car door, because if it got too hot she could just roll down the window!

Did you hear about the Table Tennis Player who broke an arm raking leaves?

Fell out of the tree"

A Table Tennis Player took a second job in a restaurant to earn some extra cash for the holidays. All went well until the boss said: "Please fill the salt shakers."

It took the Table Tennis Player three hours to put the salt through the hole in the top of the container.

Three Table Tennis Players took a small plane to the wilderness in northern Canada to hunt moose over a weekend. The pilot said: "Please remember that this is a very small plane. You can only bring back one moose between you."

But of course each Table Tennis Player killed their own moose and come Sunday, they told the pilot that last year they each brought their own moose on the plane. The pilot agreed to let them take all three dead moose home.

Just after takeoff, the plane stalled and crashed. In the wreckage, one of the Table Tennis Players woke up, looked around and said: "Where the hell are we."

"Oh, about a hundred yards east of the place where we crashed last year," replied one of the other Table Tennis Players.

Did you hear about the Table Tennis Player who lost $50 on a baseball game?

He lost another $50 on the replay.

What do you call a Table Tennis Player on a Harley wearing a leather jacket?

A rebel without a clue.

A crooked Table Tennis Player and two other prisoners escaped from jail. They ran into the woods and all hid in the trees.

When the guard shined his flashlight up the tree, the first prisoner said "meow." The guard said: "It's just a cat."

When the guard shined his flashlight up the next tree, the prisoner said: "whooo, whooo." The guard said: "It's just an owl."

When he shined his flashlight up the third tree, the Table Tennis Player said: "Moo, moo."

How many Table Tennis Player jokes are there?

None, they're all facts.

A Table Tennis Player was asked to be the Groomsman at a friend's wedding, but had to refuse because he didn't know anything about horses.

A Table Tennis Player was being honored by his peers at an award dinner, when suddenly there was a flash of light and God appeared before the Table Tennis Player.

God, turned to the Table Tennis Player and said: "You have made a great contribution to your field and I would like to reward you for everything you've done. You have the choice of infinite wealth, boundless wisdom or utter beauty. Pick one."

Without hesitating, the Table Tennis Player said: "Wisdom."

"Done!," said God, and disappeared in a cloud of smoke and a bolt of lightning.

There was a great silence as everyone looked at the Table Tennis Player. Finally, a voice called out: "Say something wise."

The Table Tennis Player turned to the crowd and said: "I should have taken the money."

There was a Table Tennis Player who sent 10 puns to friends, hoping that at least one of the puns would make them laugh. No pun in ten did.

How do you make a Table Tennis Player laugh on Monday morning?

Tell her a joke on Friday night.

Three Table Tennis Players driving from Boston to Disneyland.

After three days they arrived at their destination and turned around and went home after they saw the sign saying: "Disneyland left."

A Table Tennis Player was taken to the hospital after suffering a heart attack. While on the operating table, the Table Tennis Player had a near death experience. Seeing God, she asked: "Is my time up?"

God said: "No, you have another 15 years, 2 months and 8 days to live."

Upon recovery, the Table Tennis Player decided to get a face lift, liposuction and a tummy tuck.

Upon release from hospital, the Table Tennis Player crossed the street, was killed by a bus.

Arriving in heaven the Table Tennis Player screamed at God: "You said I had another 15 years? Why didn't you pull me from out of the bus's path?"

God replied: "I'm sorry, I didn't recognize you."

A Table Tennis Player was driving down I-95 when her cell phone rang. Her friend said: "Be careful, there's a car going the wrong way on I-95."

The Table Tennis Player replied: "They got it wrong, it's not one car, it's hundreds of them!"

Do you know how to save a drowning Table Tennis Player?

No?... Good!

A Table Tennis Player was walking down the street with a brown paper bag. He ran into one of his friends who asked what was in the bag. The Table Tennis Player said: "Fish."

The friend said if I can guess how many fish you have in the bag, you'll have to give me one."

The Table Tennis Player said: "I'll tell you what, if you can tell me how many fish I have, I'll give you both of them."

Why won't a shark attack a Table Tennis Player swimming in the ocean?

Professional courtesy.

A Table Tennis Player received a parrot as a gift. The parrot had a bad attitude and an even worse vocabulary. Every word out of the bird's mouth was rude, obnoxious and laced with profanity.

The Table Tennis Player tried to change the bird's attitude by saying only polite words, playing soft music and doing anything possible to "clean up" the bird's vocabulary.

Finally, the Table Tennis Player was fed up and yelled at the parrot. The parrot yelled back. The Table Tennis Player shook the parrot, and the parrot got angrier and angrier and ruder and ruder. In desperation, the Table Tennis Player grabbed the bird and put him in the freezer.

For a few minutes the parrot squawked and kicked and screamed. Then suddenly there was total quiet. Not a peep was heard for over a minute. Fearing that he'd hurt the parrot, the Table Tennis Player opened the door to the freezer.

The parrot calmly stepped out into the Table Tennis Player's arms and said: "I believe I may have offended you with my rude language and actions. I'm sincerely remorseful for my inappropriate transgressions and I fully intend to do everything I can to correct my rude and unforgivable behavior."

The Table Tennis Player was stunned at the change in the bird's
attitude.

As the Table Tennis Player was about to ask the parrot why he had made such a dramatic change in his behavior, the bird spoke-up, very softly and said: "May I ask what the turkey did?"

Where can you find a good Table Tennis Player?

In the cemetery.

Did you hear about the Table Tennis Player who froze to death outside a theater?

He was waiting to see the movie "Closed for the Winter."

A Table Tennis Player went out bear hunting and spotted one in the bushes and blasted away. The Table Tennis Player investigated but couldn't find the bear. As he was about to give up, he felt tap tap on his shoulder and saw the bear.

The bear said: "You know, it's not bear hunting season?"

The Table Tennis Player answered: "Yes, I know."

The bear took the rifle and smashed it on a rock, threw the hunter across a tree trunk, pulls his pants down and gave it to him. He then told the Table Tennis Player: "Get out of here. I don't want to see you again."

The Table Tennis Player was incensed, so he raced back to town and bought the biggest bear rifle he could find, and returned to the forest. A few minutes later, he spotted the bear and emptied his rifle. He then searched for the body, but couldn't find it.

He then felt a tap on his shoulder, and surprise, surprise, it was the bear again.

"I thought I told you not to come back," said the bear. The bear then proceeded to smash the new rifle, and again threw the Table Tennis Player to the ground and gave it to him again. "This is the last time I'm warning you. Don't come back."

The Table Tennis Player went berserk. When he got back to town, he bought a M16 and went straight back to the forest. Thinking he saw the bear in a bush, he took aim and emptied the entire M16. Still no body, until, a familiar tap on the shoulder.

"You're not in this for the hunting, are you?," asks the bear.

Friend: "Please close the window. It's cold outside."

Table Tennis Player: "If I close the window, will it get warm outside?"

Why did the Table Tennis Player die while drinking milk?

The cow fell on her.

A Table Tennis Player was worried that his wife was losing her hearing and he thought she might need a hearing aid. Not quite sure what to do, he called the family doctor to discuss the problem.

The doctor suggested a simple informal test that he could perform to test his wife's hearing loss. "Stand about 40 feet away from your wife," said the doctor, "and in a normal speaking voice ask her a question. If she doesn't respond, go to 30 feet, then 20 feet, and so on until you get a response."

That evening, the Table Tennis Player's wife was in the kitchen cooking dinner, and he was watching TV in the family room. He says to himself: "I'm about 40 feet away, let's see what happens."

In a normal tone he asks: 'Honey, what's for dinner?" No response. So the Table Tennis Player moved closer to the kitchen, about 30 feet from his wife and repeated the question. Still no response.

He then went into the dining room, where he was about 20 feet from his wife and asked the question a third time. Again no response.

He then walked up to the kitchen door, about 10 feet away from his wife and loudly repeated the question. Still nothing.

Finally he walks up to her and calmly says: "Honey, what's for dinner?"

"For the fifth time, we're having spaghetti," said the wife.

How do you sink a Table Tennis Player's submarine?

Knock on the hatch.

A Table Tennis Player from Montreal sent his photo to a lonely hearts club.

They wrote back saying they weren't that lonely.

A Table Tennis Player is at the post office buying stamps for her holiday cards.

"May I have 50 Chanukah stamps and 50 Christmas stamps?, said the Table Tennis Player."

The clerk asked: "What denomination?"

"Oh my god!," the woman exclaimed. "Has it really come to this? Give me 16 Orthodox, 22 Conservative and 12 Reform Chanukah cards, and 20 Catholic, 18 Greek Orthodox and 12 Lutheran Christmas stamps."

A Table Tennis Player was refused service in a restaurant. "We don't serve Table Tennis Players here," said the waiter.

That's OK said the Table Tennis Player, I don't eat Table Tennis Players."

How can you confuse a Table Tennis Player?

You can't. They're born that way.

After being married for 44 years, a Table Tennis Player took a careful look at his wife one day and said: "Darling, 44 years ago we had a cheap apartment, a junky car, slept on a sofa bed and watched a 10-inch black and white TV. But I got to sleep with a hot 21-year-old girl every night. Now I have a million dollar home, a $60,000 car, a big bed and a large-screen TV, but I'm living with a 65-year-old woman. It seems to me that you're not holding up your side of things."

The Table Tennis Player's wife replied: "No problem. If that's what you want, go for it. If you want to sleep with a 21-year-old, I'll make sure you once again get to live a cheap apartment, drive a junky car, sleep on a sofa bed and watch a 10-inch black-and-white TV!"

Did you hear about the man who wanted to be buried at sea?

His Table Tennis Player died trying to dig the grave

Why did the Table Tennis Player write TGIF on his shoes?

To remind him that Toes Go In First.

If you see a Table Tennis Player on a bicycle, why shouldn't you hit him?

He might be riding your bicycle.

A Table Tennis Player and his wife were sitting around the breakfast table one lazy Sunday morning. The Table Tennis Player turned to his wife and said: "When I die, I want you to sell all my stuff."

"Why would you want me to do that?," asked his wife.

"I figure that you'll eventually remarry, and I don't want some asshole using my stuff," replied the Table Tennis Player.

The Table Tennis Player's spouse said: "What makes you think I'd marry another asshole?"

A police officer pulled over a Table Tennis Player and asked to see
his license.

The Table Tennis Player said: "I wish you would make up your mind. Yesterday when you pulled me over you took away my license—now you want me to show it to you."

Why did God make snakes just before Table Tennis Players?

Practice.

A man walked into a bar with his alligator and asked the bartender if they served Table Tennis Players.

"Sure do," replied the bartender.

"Great," said the man. "Give me a beer, and I'll have a Table Tennis Player for my alligator."

There was a Table Tennis Player flying in a helicopter to a town 50 miles away. Suddenly everything went black.

After they crashed the pilot said: "What happened?"

The Table Tennis Player said: "I got cold, so I turned off the fan."

Ship's captain: "Please divert your course 15 degrees to the north to avoid a collision."

Table Tennis Player: "Recommend you divert your course 15 degrees to the south to avoid a collision."

Ship's captain: "This is the captain of a US Navy ship. I say again, divert your course."

Table Tennis Player: "No. I say again, you divert your course."

Ship's captain: "This is the aircraft carrier USS Lincoln, the second largest ship in the United States Atlantic fleet. We are accompanied by three destroyers, three cruisers and numerous support vessels. I demand that you change your course 15 degrees north. That's one-five degrees north, or counter measures will be undertaken to ensure the safety of this ship."

Table Tennis Player: "I'm a Table Tennis Player on vacation with my family in a lighthouse. Your call."

What's the difference between a Table Tennis Player and a bucket of dirt?

The bucket.

A Table Tennis Player and a friend were sitting in a bar, drinking beer.

The Table Tennis Player turned to his friend and said: "I'm tired of going through life being a drain on society. Tomorrow, I'm going to go down to the college and enroll in a class that will help me make society a better place."

The next day, the Table Tennis Player goes down to the college, meets the admissions officer and enrolls in a course called Logic.

At the first class, the lecturer explains that logic helps you to figure out how the world works. To demonstrate, he calls the Table Tennis Player up to the front of the classroom.

The lecturer asks: "Do you own a weed eater?"

"Yes," replies the Table Tennis Player.

"Then logically speaking, I could reasonably conclude that you have a yard," said the lecturer.

"True," said the Table Tennis Player, "I do have a yard."

The lecturer went on. "Because you have a yard, I think that you also have a house."

"That's right," said the Table Tennis Player.

"And, because you have a house, there's also a good chance that you have a family."

"Right again," said the Table Tennis Player. "I do have a family."

"I'm not done," said the lecturer. "Because you have a family, then logically you must have a wife. And, because you have a wife, logic tells me you must be a heterosexual."

"I am a heterosexual," replied the Table Tennis Player. "I'm impressed that you were able to work out so much about me without me having to say a word—just because I own a weed eater."

A couple of weeks later, the Table Tennis Player and his friend are again drinking. He tells his friend that he's studying logic, and offers to demonstrate his new-found knowledge.

The Table Tennis Player asks his friend: "Do you own a weed eater?"

"No," replied the friend.

"Then you're gay," proclaimed the Table Tennis Player.

Did you hear about the terrorists who hijacked a plane full of Table Tennis Players?

They threatened to release one each hour until their demands were met.

There was a Table Tennis Player who waited two hours at the side door of a movie theatre to see the stars come out.

A Table Tennis Player was watching the scuba divers jump off a boat when his friend turned to him and said: "Why do the scuba divers always fall backwards off the boats?"

The Table Tennis Player replied: "Because if they fell forwards they'd still be in the boat, wouldn't they?"

Four Table Tennis Players were on a plane to Las Vegas for a conference when the first Table Tennis Player said: "We've all worked together for many years, but don't really know one another. I suggest we tell each other something about ourselves that nobody knows.

They look nervously at each other, but nod OK. The first Table Tennis Player says: "Since I suggested it, I'll go first. With me it's alcohol. Every so often, I go down to a bar and drink myself silly for a few days. Not only can't I remember what I did, I have to make up an excuse to explain my absence."

They all look each other nervously, but the next Table Tennis Player slowly starts: "With me, it's gambling. Periodically, I go down to the casino and spend a couple of months salary, and then have to explain to my wife what happened. Not easy."

The third Table Tennis Player, who is really nervous, reluctantly says: "This is very difficult. With me it's women. Every so often I go down to the red light district, pick out a girl, and spend a week in the saddle. I really have problems explaining where I've been to my wife."

They all look at the fourth Table Tennis Player, waiting. He doesn't say anything. Then one of the four speaks up: "Come now, we've all told our innermost faults. It's your turn."

He looks at the others and starts hesitantly.

"Well," he says, "I'm an inveterate gossip, and I can't wait to get off this plane."

How do you confuse a Table Tennis Player?

Place three shovels against a wall and ask him to take his pick.

What is the difference between a Table Tennis Player and a pothole?

People don't run over the same pothole more than once.

A couple recently celebrated their 50th wedding anniversary and invited their three sons, all very successful Table Tennis Players, to a dinner that was being hosted by their local community to celebrate this momentous occasion.

The first son arrived 30 minutes late and said: "Happy anniversary. Sorry I'm late, but there was a lot of traffic on the freeway and I didn't have time to get you a gift."

"Not to worry," said the father. "The important thing is that we're together today."

Son number two arrived 45 minutes late and announced: "Happy anniversary. You and mom look great. I had a last minute meeting with a client, and I only just made my plane.

Sorry, but I didn't have time to shop for you."

"Don't even think about it," said the father, "we're glad you were able to come."

Five minutes later their youngest son arrived from across town and said: "Hello and happy anniversary! I'm sorry, but my boss made me work today and I was so busy packing for my vacation, I didn't have time to get you anything."

"It's fine," said the father, "at least we're all here."

After they had finished dessert, and the members of the community had dispersed, the father turned to his three Table Tennis Player children and said: "There's something your mother and I have wanted to tell you for a long time.

"When we were young, we were very poor. Despite this, we were able to send each of you to college. Throughout the years your mother and I knew that we loved each other very much, but we just never found the time to get married."

The three children gasped and son number two said: "You mean we're all bastards?"

"Yes," said the father.

"And cheap ones too."

———•———

Why did the Table Tennis Player cut a hole in his umbrella?

So he could see when it stopped raining.

———•———

Why don't they give Table Tennis Players coffee breaks?

It takes too long to retrain them.

Two Table Tennis Players went out one night and got very drunk. Thinking it wasn't a good idea to drive, they decided to walk. After a few minutes, one Table Tennis Player said: "I'm tired and drunk, I'm never going to make it home."

Since they had no money for a cab, they kept walking until they hit the bus terminal. The two Table Tennis Players looked at each other and one said: "Why don't we steal a bus?"

"Good idea," said the other.

One Table Tennis Player stood guard, and the other went inside to steal a bus. After 15 minutes, the Table Tennis Player yells: "What's happening? Haven't you found a bus yet."

The other Table Tennis Player screams back: "I can't find a 52."

"No problem," replies the other. "Just grab a 75 and we'll walk from the traffic lights."

A Table Tennis Player was telling his friend why his rent had gone up. "I told the landlord that I wanted to live in a more expensive apartment, so he raised my rent."

Why do Table Tennis Players wear slip-on shoes?

You need an IQ of at least 4 to tie a shoelace.

A Table Tennis Player was lost wandering around the desert when he came across a clothing store. Desperate for a drink, he went inside and asked the owner if he could have a glass of water.

"I'm sorry," said the store owner, "you're in the middle of the desert, I don't have any water —but I could sell you a nice tie."

"I don't need a tie," screamed the Table Tennis Player. "I need a glass of water."

Maintaining his composure, the storeowner said: "I'm sorry that I don't have any water, but over that big hill is a restaurant where you'll be able to buy food, water or any type of drink you want."

The Table Tennis Player left cursing and started walking toward
the hill.

An hour later, the totally dehydrated Table Tennis Player returned. "I'd like to buy a tie please," he said.

"What made you change your mind," asked the storeowner.

"Your brother wouldn't let me into his restaurant without a tie."

A Table Tennis Player goes to his doctor and asks for the result of the tests.

"I have bad news and worse news," says the doctor.

"Oh dear, what's the bad news?," asks the Table Tennis Player.

The doctor replies: "You only have 24 hours to live."

"That's terrible," said the Table Tennis Player. "How could the news possibly get any worse?"

The doctor replies: "I've been trying to call you since yesterday!"

What's the difference between a Table Tennis Player and a gigolo?

A gigolo only screws one person at a time.

A short balding Table Tennis Player is sitting at the bar staring at his drink when a large, trouble-making biker steps up next to him, grabs his drink and gulps it down in one swig.

"Whatcha gonna do about it?," asks the biker menacingly, as the Table Tennis Player bursts into tears.

"Come on," says the biker. "I didn't think you'd cry. I can't stand to see a man crying."

"This is the worst day of my life," said the Table Tennis Player.

"I'm a complete failure. I was late to a meeting and my boss fired me. Then I went to the parking lot and discovered that my car had been stolen and that my insurance had expired. I hailed a cab, forgot my wallet on the back seat and went home. When I got there, I found my wife in bed with another guy and my dog attacked me.

"Feeling depressed, I came to this bar to work up the courage to end it all. I bought a drink, dropped the suicide capsule in it, and sat here trying to get the nerve to swallow it, when you showed up and grabbed the drink out of my hands.

"I can't even commit suicide. It's just not my day."

A Table Tennis Player walks into the bakery and buys a cherry pie.

"Would you like it cut into four pieces or eight pieces?," asked the salesgirl.

"Better make that four pieces," said the Table Tennis Player. "I'm
on a diet."

A waiter comes over to a table full of Table Tennis Players and asks, "Is anything all right?

A Table Tennis Player owned a small ranch in Montana. The Montana Department of Labor claimed he wasn't paying his employees properly and sent an agent out to interview him.

"I need a list of your employees and the documentation showing how much you pay them," demanded the agent.

"No problem," replied the Table Tennis Player. "I have a farm hand who's been with me for three years. He earns $700 a week for 40 hours, plus free room and board.

"Then there's the cook. She's worked for me for 18 months. I pay her $550 per week for 40 hours, plus free room and board.

"Then there's the half-wit," said the Table Tennis Player. "He works at least 18 hours every day, and does 90% of the work. He makes around $50 per week and pays for his own room and board. When times are good, he gets a free bottle of bourbon on Saturday night.

"I want to meet the half-wit," says the agent.

"Pleased to make your acquaintance," replied the Table Tennis Player.

What's a definition of disappointment?

A busload of Table Tennis Players going off the edge of a cliff—with one empty seat.

One winter morning a Table Tennis Player and her husband were listening to the radio during breakfast.

The announcer came on and said: "We're expecting 8- to 10-inches of snow today. Park your car on the even-numbered side of the street, so the snowplows can get through."

Not wanting to get a ticket, the Table Tennis Player went outside and moved the car to the even-numbered side of the road.

A week later, the announcer said: "It's a miserable winter. We're expecting another 10- to 12-inches of snow today. Park your car on the odd-numbered side of the street, so the snowplows can get through."

The Table Tennis Player went out and moved her car to the odd-numbered side of the street.

The same thing happened a couple of days later when they were having breakfast, but before they could hear which side of the street to park the car, the power went out.

"What do we do now?," said the Table Tennis Player. "I have no idea where to park the car."

The husband said: "Why don't you just leave it in the garage?"

A Table Tennis Player was drinking with a few friends. After the bar closed, a drunk Table Tennis Player brought a few of his friends back to his new apartment so they could keep the party going for a couple of hours.

He took them into the living room where there was a big brass gong and a mallet.

"What's that brass gong?," one of the guests asked.

"It's not a gong, it's a talking clock," the Table Tennis Player replied.

"No way," replied his astonished friend.

"Yup," replied the drunk Table Tennis Player.

"How's it work?," the friend asked.

"Watch," the drunk Table Tennis Player replied. He picked up the mallet, gave it an ear-shattering pound and stepped back.

The three friends stood looking at one another, when all of a sudden someone on the other side of the wall screamed: "You asshole! It's 3:15 in the morning!"

What do you call a Table Tennis Player with half a brain?

Gifted.

An elderly Table Tennis Player and his wife were having dinner at another couple's house. After eating, the wives left the table and went into the kitchen to get some coffee for the men.

The two gentlemen were talking, and the Table Tennis Player said: "Last night we went to a new restaurant and it was really great. I recommend it very highly."

The other man said: "What's the name of the restaurant?"

The Table Tennis Player thought and thought and finally said: "What is the name of the flower you give to someone you love? You know, it's red and has thorns."

"You mean a rose?," asked the friend

"Yes," said the Table Tennis Player. He then yelled: "Rose, what's the name of the restaurant we went to last night?"

Why did the Table Tennis Player climb over the glass wall?

To see what was on the other side.

During a recent password audit, it was found that a Table Tennis Player was using the following password:

MickeyMinniePlutoHueyLouieDeweyDonaldGoofySacramento

When they asked the Table Tennis Player why she needed such a long password, she said she was told that it had to be eight characters long and include at least one capital.

How do you keep a Table Tennis Player busy for hours?

Write "please turn over" on both sides of a piece of paper.

How do you drive a Table Tennis Player crazy?

Give him a bag of M&Ms and tell him to alphabetize them.

A Table Tennis Player was walking to the deli along with two of his employees when he tripped over a bottle.

The Table Tennis Player picked the bottle up, rubbed the sides and a genie appeared. The genie offered each of them one wish.

"I wish I was on a beach in a tropical island," said the first employee. Immediately her wish was granted.

"I wish I was on a tour of France," said the second employee. Immediately his wish too, was granted.

It was now time for the Table Tennis Player to make his wish.

"I want my employees back in their offices right after lunch," moaned the Table Tennis Player.

What do Table Tennis Players use for birth control?

Their personalities.

A circus owner ran an ad for a lion tamer and two people showed up. One was a Table Tennis Player and the other a blonde in her mid-twenties.

The circus owner tells them: "I'm not going to sugar coat it. This is one ferocious lion. He ate my last tamer so you guys better be good or you're history. Here's your equipment—a chair, whip and a gun. Who wants to try out first?"

The girl says: "I'll go first." She walks right past the chair, the whip and the gun and steps right into the lion's cage. The lion starts to snarl and pant and begins to charge her. About half way there, she throws open her coat revealing her beautiful naked body. The lion stops dead in his tracks, sheepishly crawls up to her and starts licking her feet and ankles. He continues to lick and kiss her entire body for several minutes and then rests his head on her feet.

The circus owner's mouth is on the floor. He says: "I've never seen a display like that in my life." He then turns to the Table Tennis Player and asks: "Can you top that?"

The Table Tennis Player replies: "No problem, just get that lion out of the way."

A Table Tennis Player was sitting in a bar having a drink and watching the 10 o'clock news. There was a story about a man on a ledge of a building preparing to jump came on. The Table Tennis Player turns to the customer next to him asked: "Do you think he'll jump?"

The customer says: "I bet he'll jump."

The Table Tennis Player says: "I bet you $20 he won't."

Just as the customer placed her money on the bar, the guy jumped off of the building, falling to his death.

The Table Tennis Player handed his $20 to the customer and said: "All's fair. Here's your money."

The customer replies: "I can't take your money. I saw the 6 o'clock news and knew he'd jump."

"So did I," said the Table Tennis Player, "but I didn't think he'd do it again."

Did you hear about the Table Tennis Player who locked his keys in his car?

He needed a coat hanger to get his family out.

Three friends went down to Mexico one night, got drunk, and woke up in jail, only to find that they were to be executed in the morning. Unfortunately, none of them could remember what they did the night before.

The first friend was strapped in the electric chair, and was asked if she had any last words.

She said: "I believe in the almighty power of God to intervene on the behalf of the innocent." The prison warden threw the switch and nothing happened.

Immediately, the prison warden begs her for forgiveness, and sets her free.

The second friend is strapped in and says: "I am a law student and I believe in the power of justice to intervene on the part of the innocent." They threw the switch again, nothing happened.

The prison warden begs her for forgiveness, and releases her.

The last one, a Table Tennis Player, is strapped in and says: "Before I became a Table Tennis Player, I was an electrician, and I can tell you right now, you're not going to electrocute anybody if you don't plug this thing in."

A Table Tennis Player was on a United flight to Australia and the flight attendant asked him if he wanted any dinner.

"What are my choices?," asked the Table Tennis Player.

"Yes or no," replied the flight attendant.

What's the difference between a Table Tennis Player and a vulture?

Vultures wait until you're dead to rip your heart out.

The Table Tennis Player was sitting in a fine restaurant with his wife when she looked over at a nearby table and saw a man in a drunken stupor.

The Table Tennis Player said: "You've been watching that man for some time now. Do you know him?"

"Yes," replied the wife. "He's my ex-husband. He's been drinking like that since I left him seven years ago."

"That's amazing," the Table Tennis Player replies, "I didn't think anybody could celebrate for that long."

Did you hear about the lion walking through the woods eating deer droppings?

He had just eaten a Table Tennis Player and was trying to get the taste out of his mouth!

A Table Tennis Player walked into a bar and ordered martini after martini, each time removing the olives and placing them in a jar.

When the jar was filled with olives, the Table Tennis Player got up to leave.

"Excuse me," said a customer, who was puzzled over what the Table Tennis Player had done. "Why did you put all the olives from your drinks in the jar?"

The Table Tennis Player replied: "My wife just sent me out for a
jar of olives!"

What do Table Tennis Players and sperm have in common?

A sperm has one-in-3 million chance of actually becoming a human being.

Three friends were stumbling home from a bar one night and found themselves on the road which led past the old cemetery.

"Come have a look over here," said one friend. "It's Michael Rosenbaum's grave. He lived to the ripe old age of 87."

"That's nothing," said the second friend. "Here's one named Patrick Bradley, it says here that he was 95 when he died."

Just then, the Table Tennis Player yells out: "Good God, here's a guy who lived to be 145!"

"What was his name?," asks friend number two.

The Table Tennis Player stumbles, and awkwardly lights a

match to see what else is written on the stone marker, and exclaims: "It's Miles, from Dallas."

How do you get a Table Tennis Player to laugh at a joke on Saturday?

Tell it to him on Wednesday.

A Table Tennis Player needed a vacation and decided that ice fishing was what he needed to relieve his tension.

After arriving at his destination a couple of days later, he started to drill, when all of a sudden he heard a loud booming voice yelling: "There's no fish down there."

He stopped, moved over a few feet and started drilling for a second time. Again, he heard the loud booming voice yelling: "There's no fish down there."

So the Table Tennis Player moved over about 50 feet and started to drill for the third time. The same loud booming voice again broke the silence and said: "There's no fish there either."

Getting nervous, the Table Tennis Player looked around, saw nobody and asked: "Who are you? God?"

"No," replied the booming voice. "I'm the ice skating arena manager."

What do you call 25 skydiving Table Tennis Players?

Skeet.

A Table Tennis Player and his friend were both patients in a mental hospital. One day, while they were walking around the hospital's swimming pool, his friend jumped into the pool and promptly sank to the bottom.

Thinking quickly, the Table Tennis Player jumped in and pulled his friend out.

When the medical director heard about the Table Tennis Player's heroic act, he immediately ordered him released as he was considered mentally stable.

When he went to tell the Table Tennis Player the news he said: "I have good news and bad news. The good news is you're being discharged, as you were able to rationally respond to a crisis by jumping in and saving your friend's life.

"The bad news is that your friend hung himself in the bathroom with his bathrobe belt right after you saved him."

The Table Tennis Player said: "He didn't hang himself, I hung him there to dry. How soon can I go home?"

What's the difference between a dead skunk on the road and a dead Table Tennis Player on the road?

Vultures will eat the skunk.

A Table Tennis Player walks into a bar. The bartender asks: "What will you have?"

The Table Tennis Player says: "Give me three pints of beer, please."

So the bartender brings him three pints and the man proceeds to alternately sip one, then the other, then the third until they're gone. He then orders three more.

The bartender says: "I know you like them cold. You don't have to order three at a time. I can keep an eye on it, and when you're low, bring you a fresh cold one."

"You don't understand," said the Table Tennis Player. "I have two brothers, one in Dallas and one in Nevada. We made a vow to each other that every Saturday night we'd still drink together. So right now, each of my brothers has three beers, and we're drinking together."

The bartender thought that was a wonderful tradition.

Every week the man came in and ordered three beers. Then one week he came in and ordered only two. He drank them and then ordered two more.

"I know your tradition," said the bartender. "And I'd just like to let you know that I'm sorry one of your brothers died."

"My brothers are fine," said the Table Tennis Player. "I only ordered two beers because I've quit drinking."

A Table Tennis Player was working on a construction site to earn extra cash. The boss needed a wheelbarrow. A short time later the Table Tennis Player returned with two wheelbarrows, one on top of another.

The boss said: "I only wanted one."

The Table Tennis Player said: "What did you want me to do, carry it?"

A Table Tennis Player was flying to New York in a four-engine plane, when the pilot announced that one engine had failed and there would be a 30-minute delay. The pilot said there was no reason for concern as the jet had three more engines. The same announcement was made two more times.

Finally, the Table Tennis Player turned to the person in the next seat and said: "I hope the other engine doesn't fail, or we'll be up here all day."

What's the difference between a Table Tennis Player and a trampoline?

You take off your shoes before you jump on a trampoline.

A Table Tennis Player was touring Europe in a chauffeur-driven Mercedes-Benz. The Table Tennis Player asked the driver what the emblem on the front of the car was for.

The driver said it was to line up parking inspectors. Nothing else was said until they saw a parking inspector writing tickets.

The Table Tennis Player asked the driver to demonstrate the device. The driver carefully lined up the parking inspector and went straight for him—swerving at the last minute.

Suddenly there was a loud bang. "What happened?," asked the driver.

"The Table Tennis Player said: "You would have missed him if I hadn't opened the door."

An elderly Table Tennis Player is hit by a car and brought to the hospital.

The nurse asks: "Are you comfortable, sir?"

The Table Tennis Player replied: "I make a living."

A Table Tennis Player hired a plumber to do a couple of jobs around his house. When he received the bill he was angry to find he had been charged $350 an hour.

The Table Tennis Player said: "I'm a highly paid professional and
I don't earn that much.

The plumber said: "Neither did I when I was a
highly paid professional. "

Did you hear the sad story about the Table Tennis Player who was given a pill that was supposed to radically increase a person's IQ. When it was given to rats, they were able to run a maze with one eye closed in half the time it took the other rats to complete the course.

Needless to say, the doctors were anxious to try it out on humans. When approval was granted, they gave it to several people including a Table Tennis Player, who took it faithfully every day.

Two years later, the Table Tennis Player earned a degree in brain surgery—an all time record.

Unfortunately, the Table Tennis Player was part of the control group that had been given a placebo. There he was, dumb as ever, and stuck with a medical degree. What a waste. Really sad.

A Table Tennis Player was sitting at a bar when he notices a lamp on the bookshelf. He wanders over and begins to rub it.

Out pops a genie and offers him three wishes. Immediately he says I want a glass of beer that automatically refills itself.

A glass of beer appears. The Table Tennis Player drinks it quickly, and it immediately refills itself. He does the same thing two more times.

The genie then asks what he wants for his other two wishes.

Without thinking, the Table Tennis Player says quickly: "I'll take another two of these."

Two Table Tennis Players were driving to their new jobs in Florida, when they saw a sign which said "Clean bathrooms."

By the time they had reached Florida, they had cleaned 32 bathrooms.

A Table Tennis Player and another person applied for a part-time job waitressing to earn some extra money. Being a high-class establishment, the owner of the bar gave them both a 10 question test to determine who should get the job.

Both applicants handed in the test, and they both correctly answered the first nine questions.

The bar owner then went up to the Table Tennis Player and said: "You both got question 10 wrong, but based on the way you answered the question, I've decided to hire the other person.

"What do you mean?," said the Table Tennis Player. "How could one wrong answer be better than another wrong answer?"

"Simple," replied the bar owner. "On question 10, the other applicant wrote: 'I don't know,' and you wrote 'neither do I.'"

What is the first thing you should do if you find a Table Tennis Player buried up to his neck in cement?

Get more cement.

A young, Table Tennis Player was walking around a field in Long Island, when he came across an old lamp. He rubbed the lamp and suddenly a genie appeared before him.

"For freeing me, I will grant you one wish," said the genie.

"I wish that there was a bridge from New York to London so I don't get ripped off every time I go on vacation," said the Table Tennis Player.

"I'm sorry, but I can't do that," said the genie. "It would be too much change. Thousands of people would be put out of work. Government revenue would be reduced dramatically. It would mess up too many people's lives."

So the Table Tennis Player thought for a second and said: "OK, then. I'm a Table Tennis Player, and I'm tired of everyone making fun of me. I wish that Table Tennis Players were as smart, or smarter than everyone else in the world."

The genie said: "Would you like two lanes, or four?"

Three Table Tennis Players were waiting to be interviewed for a job. The first Table Tennis Player was called into the office, and after the normal questions was told that he would have to answer a question that tested his verbal skills.

The interviewer said: "I would like you to make a sentence using the word 'sweater.'"

The Table Tennis Player said: "My mother knitted me a sweater."

"I'll get back to you," said the interviewer. "Please ask the next applicant to come in."

After the second Table Tennis Player's interview he also was asked make a sentence using the word "sweater."

The second Table Tennis Player said: "My mother knitted me a sweater."

Of course, the interviewer was suspicious, but he told the Table Tennis Player that he would get back to him.

Getting wise, the interviewer changed the question for the third Table Tennis Player. Instead of asking him to use the word "sweater," he asked him to use "fascinate."

The Table Tennis Player said: "My mother knitted me a nice sweater with 10 buttons, but I can only fasten eight."

How can you tell if a Table Tennis Player is lying?

His lips are moving.

A Table Tennis Player returned home one night when he came across a dead body on his lawn. Thinking quickly, he called 911 and reported the incident.

"Where's the body," asked the 911 operator.

"It's at the end of Eucalyptus Drive," the Table Tennis Player replied.

"Could you please spell that for me?," the operator asked.

After a long pause, the Table Tennis Player said: "How about if I drag the body over to Oak Street and you pick it up there?"

What's the difference between a Table Tennis Player and a vampire?

A vampire only sucks blood at night.

A Table Tennis Player was walking down the street with a case of beer under his arm when his friend Peter stopped him and asked what he got the case of beer for.

"I got it for my partner," replied the Table Tennis Player.

"Good trade," replied Peter.

A Table Tennis Player and two of his friends walked into a bar and ordered three beers.

Just as they were about to take a drink, three flies appeared and jumped into each glass.

The first friend pushed away the beer in disgust. The second friend scooped the fly out of the beer and started drinking as if nothing had happened.

The Table Tennis Player picked the fly out of his drink and started shaking it over his drink and began yelling: "Spit it out. Come on already, spit it out."

What's black and brown and looks good on a Table Tennis Player?

A Doberman pinscher.

What's the difference between a dead skunk on the road and a dead Table Tennis Player on the road?

Skid marks in front of the skunk.

You are in a room with a mass murderer, a terrorist and a Table Tennis Player.

You have a gun with only two bullets.

What do you do?

Shoot the Table Tennis Player twice.

A Table Tennis Player dies and goes to hell. The devil greets him warmly at the gates, and as they enter a long corridor, the devil explains that the Table Tennis Player must choose a room where he will spend eternity.

As they approach the first room, the door opens, and the Table Tennis Player peers in. There's an endless circle of people standing on hot coals with weights strapped to their backs.

"I don't think I want to spend eternity here," said the Table Tennis Player.

The devil then showed the Table Tennis Player the second room.

In this room, the damned walk around on broken glass listening to elevator music.

"This isn't much fun," said the Table Tennis Player. "I definitely don't want to spend any more time in this room."

In the last room, the Table Tennis Player was surprised to find the damned standing around up to their armpits in vomit drinking coffee.

"That doesn't look so bad!," said the Table Tennis Player. "I'll stay here."

"Very well," said the Devil, closing the door behind him.

"Suddenly, the room supervisor called out on his megaphone: "Alright everybody, coffee break's over. Back on your heads."

What do you call 100 Table Tennis Players at the bottom of the ocean?

A good start.

Santa Claus, the tooth fairy, an honest Table Tennis Player and an old drunk are walking down the street together when they simultaneously spot a hundred dollar bill.

Who gets it?

The old drunk, of course. The other three are mythical creatures.

How do you save a drowning Table Tennis Player?

Throw him a rock.

A rich man who was very close to his money got together with his Table Tennis Player and two of his friends. He then announced and that he was dying and had less than a month to live.

He handed each person an envelope with $100,000 in it and asked everyone to do him a favor after he died.

"Each of these envelopes contains $100,000," said the rich man. "Since I don't want to go to the afterlife without my money, would you please throw these envelopes into my coffin after I die?"

Every one in the group agreed, and took the envelopes.

About a month later, the rich man died and the group reconvened at the funeral.

As promised, each man threw his envelope into the coffin before it was closed up.

As they were leaving, the first friend said: "I have a confession to make. My local church needed a new altar, so I took $5,000 out of the envelope and bought it."

The next friend looked at his feet and said: "Since we're coming clean, I thought it was a waste of money to bury all of the money in the coffin, so I took $30,000 out of the envelope and bought the hospital a new X-ray machine.

Both men then looked at the Table Tennis Player, expecting him to also make a confession. "You guys are crooks," said the Table Tennis Player. "I didn't take any money. I put a check in the coffin for the entire $100,000."

A Table Tennis Player rang United and asked how long it took to fly from New York to Chicago.

"Just a minute, sir," said the United reservations clerk.

"Thank you," said the Table Tennis Player and hung up.

A man walked into a bar and asked the barman if he had heard the latest Table Tennis Player joke.

"I'm warning you," said the Table Tennis Player loudly, "I'm a Table Tennis Player who's just working part-time as a Table Tennis Player to make some extra money."

"That's all right," said the man. "I'll tell it slowly."

A man hired an unemployed Table Tennis Player as his office assistant. On the first day the phone rang, and the Table Tennis Player hung up immediately.

"Who was that?," asked the boss.

"Some fool saying it was long distance from Brazil," replied the Table Tennis Player. "I told him everybody knew that."

What's the difference between a Table Tennis Player and an onion?

People cry when they cut up an onion.

How do you get a Table Tennis Player out of a tree?

Cut the rope.

Why do Table Tennis Players always carry garbage in their pockets?

Identification.

A Table Tennis Player attended a show where a ventriloquist who fancied himself as a comedian told 20 Table Tennis Player jokes in a row.

"Look," shouted the Table Tennis Player, standing up in the audience. "I'm fed up being insulted by all these jokes. Table Tennis Players are not as stupid as you make out."

"Sit down," said the ventriloquist. "They're only jokes. Don't tell me that Table Tennis Players haven't got a sense of humor."

"Be quiet," said the Table Tennis Player. "I'm not talking to you. "I'm talking to the little fellow on your knee."

A man walks into a bar and says: "I hear Table Tennis Players are a bunch of hard drinkers. I'll bet $500 to anybody who can drink 20 glasses of whisky back-to-back."

The room is quiet, and no one takes up the man's bet. One person leaves.

Thirty minutes later the person who left returns, and taps the man on the shoulder: "Is your bet still on?," asks the Table Tennis Player.

"Yes," says the man and as he asks the Table Tennis Player to line up 20 glasses of whisky. Immediately the Table Tennis Player tears into all 20 glasses, and drinks them back-to-back.

The other pub patrons cheer as the man hands over the $500 to Table Tennis Player and says: "Why did you leave the bar before, instead of taking up my challenge when I offered it?"

The Table Tennis Player said: "$500 is a lot of money, so I went to the bar down the street to see if I could do it first."

What do you call a Table Tennis Player sitting on the grass?

Fertilizer.

A priest died and went to heaven. When he got there, he found a Table Tennis Player in line in front of him at the Pearly Gates. Saint Peter came over and said to the priest: "Just a minute, I'll be right back," as he took the Table Tennis Player away to his room.

A few minutes later he returned and said to the priest: "Follow me to your new quarters."

Along the way, they passed many people in their heavenly abodes, including the Table Tennis Player's quarters.

The priest was awe-struck by the opulence and splendor of the Table Tennis Player's quarters. There were fine silks, rare foods and drinks, soft music, and attractive young women to serve him for eternity.

The priest finally arrived at his new quarters—a small 6-foot by 9-foot room with bare walls, a plain bed and a Bible for entertainment. The priest said: "I don't want to sound ungrateful, but how come the Table Tennis Player gets a magnificent room and I get this dump."

Saint Peter smiled and said: "We have a lot of priests here in heaven, but only one Table Tennis Player."

Did you hear about the Table Tennis Player who spent four days in Macy's looking for wheels for a miscarriage?

A Table Tennis Player and his friend were repairing a barn roof, when suddenly a strong wind blew and knocked their ladder down. Since there was no help nearby, both men decided to jump.

Looking around for something that would break their fall, they saw a pile of manure. The Table Tennis Player jumped first.

"Are you alright?," asked his friend.

"How deep is it?"

The Table Tennis Player answers: "I'm fine. It's only up to my knees."

"Great. Here I come," yelled the friend as he lands in a pile of manure up to his neck.

You said it was only up to your knees," cried the friend.

"It did only come up to my knees," said the Table Tennis Player. "I jumped head first."

Hear the one about the deaf Table Tennis Player?

Neither did he.

One day a Table Tennis Player was sitting on a beach when he saw a young woman swimming far out to sea. As he watched, he saw a shark circling her. Immediately, he jumped into the water, karate chopped the shark, killed it instantly, and helped the young woman swim to the beach.

After he got back to the beach, a journalist ran up to him and said: "That was the most courageous thing I've ever seen. I'm going to let the world know about this. You'll be famous. I can see the headline now: 'Man Saves Girl From Killer Shark.'"

"What do you do for a living?"

"I'm a Table Tennis Player," replied the man of the moment.

"Great," said the journalist. "You'll see the story in tomorrow's paper."

The next day, the Table Tennis Player bought the paper and the headline read: "Table Tennis Player Kills Girl's Pet."

A young Table Tennis Player decided to turn his life over to God and thought that the best way to do this was to become a monk, so he checked himself into a monastery.

At his indoctrination the head monk told him that they were sworn to TOTAL silence—but every 10 years they were permitted to speak two words.

After 10 years of total silence, the head monk indicated it was now time for the former Table Tennis Player to speak his two words.

The monk said: "Bed hard," and then resumed his silent study and work.

Another 10 years passed, and the head monk again indicated it was time for him to speak his two words.

The monk said: "Food bad," and the former Table Tennis Player then resumed his silent study and work.

Thirty years after entering the monastery, it was again time for the former Table Tennis Player to speak, this time he said: "I quit."

The head monk shook his head and said: "I knew this was coming. You've done nothing but complain for the past 30 years!"

Did you hear about the Table Tennis Player who was asked to be a Jehovah's Witness?

He refused because he didn't see the accident.

A Table Tennis Player went to his doctor and said he had a serious problem because he could never remember what he said.

"When did you first notice this problem?," asked the doctor.

"What problem?," asked the Table Tennis Player.

A Table Tennis Player was jumping up and down on the floor yelling and screaming when a friend walked into the room.

"What's wrong?," asked the friend.

"Nothing, nothing at all," relied the Table Tennis Player. "I'm just so happy. I finished a jigsaw puzzle in record time."

"How long did it take you?, asked the friend."

"Six months," replied the Table Tennis Player. "On the box it said three to five years."

Not all Table Tennis Players are bad, but it's a crying shame that the other ninety-nine percent make the rest look bad.

A drunk climbs on a bar stool in a bar and screams: "All Table Tennis Players are thieves."

A man stands up and says: "I resent that remark."

The drunk shouts back: "Are you a Table Tennis Player?" "No," says the man "I'm a thief."

A Table Tennis Player and his wife in their 60s were visited by a fairy who granted them both a wish.

"I want to travel round the world with my darling husband," said the Table Tennis Player's wife.

Two tickets for a luxury cruise magically appeared in her hand.

A couple of minutes later the Table Tennis Player said: "Sorry, but my wish is to have a wife 30 years younger than me."

The fairy waved her wand, and suddenly he was 92.

Did you hear about the Table Tennis Players' Rubik's cube?

It's white on all sides and it takes two seconds to solve.

A Table Tennis Player went to a pet shop and asked how many budgie birds were in stock. "We have 99 birds," replied the shop owner. "I'll take them all," said the Table Tennis Player. He went to a tailor and had 99 pockets sewn into his jacket. He then put a budgie bird in each pocket and went up to the top of the tallest building in town and jumped off.

The Table Tennis Player hit the ground with an almighty smack and lay there groaning until a person passed by and asked him what had happened. "I don't know," replied the Table Tennis Player. "But that's the last time I try budgie jumping."

Two Table Tennis Players were walking home one night after drinking when a severed head rolled along the ground in front of them.

The first Table Tennis Player picked it up, and asked if it was their good friend Mike. "No," said the second Table Tennis Player: "Mike was taller than that."

An unemployed Table Tennis Player got a job at a sawmill. Just before lunch, he yelled: "Dave, I lost my finger."

"How did you do it?," asked Dave.

"I just touched this big spinning thing here, like thi...," replied the Table Tennis Player.

"Darn! There goes another one!," yelled the Table Tennis Player.

How do you brainwash a Table Tennis Player?

Give him an enema.

A Table Tennis Player opened her morning newspaper and was dumbfounded to read in the obituary column that her best friend Susan had died. Before she could do anything, the phone rang. It was Susan.

"Did you see my obituary in today's newspaper?," asked Susan. "It said I died!!"

"Of course I saw it," replied the Table Tennis Player. "Where are you calling from?"

What do you have when a Table Tennis Player is buried up to his neck in sand?

Not enough sand.

A Table Tennis Player was staggering home after a hard night of drinking with a bottle of wine in his back pocket when he slipped and fell badly. Struggling to his feet, the Table Tennis Player felt something wet running down his leg.

"Please, God," implored the Table Tennis Player, "let it be blood!"

A Table Tennis Player went to trial for armed robbery when the jury foreman came out and announced: "Not guilty."

"That's great," shouted the Table Tennis Player.

"Does that mean I can keep the money?," the Table Tennis Player asked the judge.

What does a Table Tennis Player say when you blow in his ear?

"Thanks for the refill!"

A Table Tennis Player phoned the maternity ward. "Quick," he said. "Send an ambulance, my wife is having a baby!"

"Tell me, is this her first baby?," the doctor asked.

"No, this is her husband Kevin," replied the Table Tennis Player.

A Table Tennis Player and his friend were catching the subway late one night when they came across a notice stating: "Dogs Must Be Carried On the Escalator."

"Great," said the Table Tennis Player to his friend. "Where am I going to find a dog at this time of night?"

Two mothers were bragging about their sons.

The first said: "My son is such a saint. He studied hard, got himself a degree, doesn't smoke, and he hasn't so much as looked at a woman in over two years."

The Table Tennis Player's mother responds: "My son is also quite a saint. He studied hard, became a Table Tennis Player and not only hasn't he not looked at a woman in more than three years, but he hasn't touched any liquor in all that time."

"My word," said the first mother. "You must be so proud."

"I am," said the Table Tennis Player's mother. "And, when he gets out of jail, I'm going to throw him a huge party."

Table Tennis Player: "My dog fell down a hole and I had to shoot it."

Friend: "Did you shoot it in the hole?"

Table Tennis Player: "No, in the head."

A Table Tennis Player, wanting to earn some money, decided to hire herself out as a handyman and started canvassing a wealthy neighborhood.

She went to the front door of the first house and asked the owner if he had any jobs for her to do.

"Well, you can paint my porch," replied the homeowner. "How much will you charge?"

The Table Tennis Player said, "How about $50?"

The homeowner agreed and told her that the paint and ladders were in the garage.

The homeowner's wife heard the conversation and asked her husband: "Does she realize that the porch goes all the way around the house?"

"She should," said the homeowner. "She was on the porch."

A short time later, the Table Tennis Player came to the door to collect her money.

"You're finished already?," the homeowner asked.

"Yes," the Table Tennis Player answered. "Since I had some paint left over, I decided to give it two coats."

Impressed, the homeowner reached in his pocket for the $50.

"And by the way," the Table Tennis Player added, "It's not a Porch, it's a Ferrari."

What do you call a Table Tennis Player with two brain cells?

Pregnant.

Two Table Tennis Players won $5,000,000 in a lottery. While having a drink one night, the first Table Tennis Player said to the second Table Tennis Player:

"What are we going to do about the begging letters?"

The second Table Tennis Player said:

"We're going to continue sending them out?"

Hear about the Table Tennis Player who got stuck in a bear trap?

Chewed off both arms and one leg and still couldn't get away.

A broke Table Tennis Player decides to ask God for help.

"Dear Lord," he prays. "If I don't get some cash, I'm going to lose everything. Please let me win the lottery."

Lottery night comes, but the Table Tennis Player doesn't win.

He prays even harder, saying: "God, why have you forsaken me? My children are starving. Please just let me win."

Suddenly there is a blinding flash of light, and the Table Tennis Player hears God speak.

"Work with me on this," God says. "Buy a ticket."

How do you keep a Table Tennis Player happy in his old age?

Tell him jokes when he's young.

A Table Tennis Player walks into a doctor's office and tells the doctor she's broken every single bone in her body.

"That's impossible," says the doctor.

The Table Tennis Player says: "It's true. Look!" She then touches her leg with her index finger and screams: "Ouch!"

Then she touches her arm and yells: "Eeeeoooow!"

Finally she touches her ribs and can barely maintain her composure as the tears start to roll down her face.

"See, I told you I broke every bone in my body," she said.

The doctor rubs his chin, then conducts a thorough examination.

"Well, Miss," he tells her, "I've got some good news and some bad news. The good news is, you haven't broken every bone in your body. The bad news is, you've broken your finger."

An executive was interviewing a Table Tennis Player for a position in his company. He wanted to find out something about her personality so he asked: "If you could have a conversation with someone, living or dead, who would it be?"

The Table Tennis Player quickly responded, "The living one."

How do you tell who the Table Tennis Player is on an oil drilling
platform?

He's the one throwing bread to the helicopters.

Did you hear about the Table Tennis Player who took a roll of toilet paper to a crap game?

"So, have you figured what to buy your wife for the holidays?," asked Sam.

"I sure have," replied the Table Tennis Player.

"My wife made it easy. She said she wanted something with diamonds, so I bought her a deck of cards."

———

A Table Tennis Player returned home from work early one day and found his wife in bed with another man.

Upset, he grabbed his gun and pointed it at his head, which made his wife burst out laughing.

"What are you laughing at," cried the Table Tennis Player. "You're next.

———

How many Table Tennis Players does it take to screw in a light bulb?

How many can you afford?

———

An unemployed Table Tennis Player and his wife moved to a farm to reduce costs and work out what to do while the economy recovered. Their modest house had no running water or electricity.

Nine months after they moved, the Table Tennis Player's wife's water broke and the doctor arrived.

"What do you want me to do, doctor?," asked the Table Tennis Player.

"Hold the lantern. Here it comes," said the doctor as he held up child for all to see.

"Congratulations, you're the proud father of a ...," said the doctor.

Before he could finish his sentence, the doctor said: "Wait a minute. Hold the lantern," and the doctor delivered a beautiful baby daughter to the Table Tennis Player and his wife.

A couple of minutes later he again shouted: "Hold the lantern," and moments later held up a third baby.

"Doctor," asks the Table Tennis Player, "Do you think it's the light that's attracting them?"

A cop pulls over two Table Tennis Players who were very, very drunk.

He says to the first: "What is your name and address?"

The Table Tennis Player replies: "I'm Mark Johnstone of no fixed address."

The cop turns to the second Table Tennis Player, and asks the same question.

"I'm David Harris, and I live in the apartment above Mark."

A drunk Table Tennis Player gets on a bus and asks the conductor how long the trip is between New York and Boston.

"About four hours, depending on traffic," said the driver.

"Okay," says the drunk. "How long is the trip between Boston and New York?"

The bus driver says to the Table Tennis Player: "It's still about four hours. Why do you think there'd be a difference?"

"Well," says the drunk Table Tennis Player: "It's only a week between Christmas and New Year, but it's a lot longer between New Year and Christmas!"

How do you save a drowning Table Tennis Player?

Take your foot off his head.

Why did the Table Tennis Player put dynamite in his trunk?

In case he needed to blow up his tires.

A Table Tennis Player and his two friends were about to go down the waterslide when a wrinkled old man steps in front of them.

"This is a magic ride," says the wrinkled old man. "You will land in whatever you shout out on the way down."

"I'm game," said the first friend and shouted "Gold," at the top of his voice as he slid down the slide. When he hit the bottom he found himself surrounded by thousands of gold coins.

The next friend shouted "Silver" at the top of her voice, and landed in more silver coinage than she knew what to do with.

The Table Tennis Player went last and, launching himself from the top of the slide shouted "weeee!"

Why do they bury Table Tennis Players 20 feet deep after they die?

Because deep down they are really nice people.

How do you get a Table Tennis Player to climb on the roof of a bar?

Tell him drinks are on the house!

A Table Tennis Player lived with his dog for many years, and when the dog died, he went to his local parish priest and asked if services could be said for his dog.

The priest said: "No, we can't have services for a dog here, but that new church down the street that might be willing to do it."

"Thank you," said the Table Tennis Player. "Do you think $50,000 is a big enough donation?"

"Why didn't you tell me the dog was Catholic?," said the priest.

What's the difference between Table Tennis Players and pigs?

Pigs don't turn into Table Tennis Players when they drink.

A Table Tennis Player had just finished reading a book titled, You Can Be The Man of Your House."

He stormed into the kitchen and said to his wife: "From now on, you need to know that I am the man of this house and my word is law. You will prepare me a gourmet meal tonight, and when I'm done eating, you'll serve me a scrumptious dessert.

And, after dinner, you're going to go upstairs with me and we will have the kind of sex that I want. "Then, you're going to draw me a bath, wash my back and towel me dry and bring me my robe. Then, you'll massage my feet and hands. Then tomorrow, guess who's going to dress me and comb my hair?"

The Table Tennis Player's wife replied: "The funeral director?"

What's the difference between a Table Tennis Player and a computer?

You only have to punch information into a computer once.

Did you hear about the Table Tennis Player who studied all night for his blood test.

Why do Table Tennis Players hate M&Ms?

They're too hard to peel.

What do you call a Table Tennis Player who scores well in an IQ test?

A cheat.

There was a Table Tennis Player who worked hard all his life and saved all of his money, refusing to part with any of it except for essentials.

On his deathbed, the Table Tennis Player turned to his wife and said: "When I die, I want you to take all my money and put it in the casket with me so I take it to afterlife with me."

His wife faithfully promised to carry out his last wish and agreed to put all of his money into the casket with him.

At the funeral, the service was held and just before they closed the casket, his wife shouted: "Wait a moment, and quickly put a metal box in the casket next to the Table Tennis Player. The undertaker closed the casket down and rolled it away.

The wife's friend turned to her and said: "Girl, I knew you weren't foolish enough to put all of his money in the coffin, what was in the box?"

The Table Tennis Player's wife replied: I promised to put his money in the casket and I can't go back on my word.

"You mean to tell say, you me you put all of his money in the coffin?," said the friend.

"You bet I did," said the Table Tennis Player's wife. "I withdrew all his money from his bank account, put it in my checking account and wrote him a check. If he can cash it, then he can spend it."

A Table Tennis Player is someone who thinks the three major political parties are Republican, Democratic and Cocktail.

A Table Tennis Player walks into the bar and says to the bartender: "I'll bet you $200 I can pee into that glass on the top shelf without spilling a drop."

The Table Tennis Player contemplates this and says: "You're on."

So the Table Tennis Player drops his pants and pees all over the bar. When he's finished the only dry spot left is the top shelf.

The bar tender is beside himself with laughter, but stops laughing when he sees the Table Tennis Player laughing his head off.

"Why are you laughing?," he asks the Table Tennis Player, "You've just lost $200."

"Yes," said the Table Tennis Player. "I did lose $200, but I bet the guys outside $1,000 that I could pee all over your bar and you'd be laughing."

Why do Table Tennis Players drive BMWs?

Because they can't spell Porsche.

A Table Tennis Player boards a plane to New York with a ticket for the economy section. She looks at the seats in economy and then looks into the front cabin at the first-class seats.

Seeing that the first-class seats are larger and more comfortable, the Table Tennis Player takes the last empty one.

The flight attendant checks her ticket and asks the Table

Tennis Player to move back to her seat in economy.

The Table Tennis Player refuses.

Flustered, the flight attendant goes to the cockpit and informs the captain of the problem.

The captain goes back and tells the woman that her assigned seat is in economy.

The Table Tennis Player again refuses to move.

The captain doesn't want to cause a commotion, and so he returns to the cockpit to discuss the problem with the copilot.

The copilot says that his girlfriend is a Table Tennis Player, and that he can take care of the problem.

He then goes back and briefly whispers something in the Table Tennis Player's ear.

She immediately gets up, says: "Thank you so much," hugs the copilot, and rushes back to her seat in economy.

The pilot and flight attendant, who were watching with rapt attention, together ask the copilot what he had said to the Table Tennis Player.

He replies, "I just told her that the first class section wasn't going to New York."

What do you call a fly in a Table Tennis Player's head?

Space invader.

A man gets a call from his Table Tennis Player friend.

"I've got a problem," says the Table Tennis Player.

"What's the matter?," asks the friend.

"Well, I've bought this jigsaw puzzle, but it's too hard. None of the pieces fit together and I can't find any edges," said the Table Tennis Player.

"What's the picture of?," asks the friend.

"It's of a big rooster," replies the Table Tennis Player.

"All right," says the friend. "I'll come over and have a look."

As he gets to the Table Tennis Player's house, he goes into the kitchen and finds the pieces on the kitchen table.

The friend looks at the jigsaw and then turns to the Table Tennis Player and says: "For Pete's sake—put the cornflakes back in the box."

Why do Table Tennis Players' lunchboxes have clear lids?

So they can tell if it's morning or afternoon.

A Table Tennis Player goes to Australia for a vacation. There he meets an Aussie farmer and gets talking.

The Aussie shows off his wheat field and the Table Tennis Player says: "Oh! We have wheat fields that are twice as large."

Then they walk around the farm and the Aussie shows off his herd of cattle.

The Table Tennis Player immediately says: "We have longhorns that are at least twice as large as your cows."

The conversation has almost died when the Table Tennis Player sees a herd of kangaroos hopping through the field.

The Table Tennis Player asks: "And what are those?"

The Aussie gives the Table Tennis Player an incredulous look and asks: "Don't you have any grasshoppers where you come from?"

What's the difference between yoghurt and a Table Tennis Player?

Yoghurt has a little culture.

What's a Table Tennis Player's idea of safe sex?

Locking the car doors.

Did you hear about the Table Tennis Player who saw a notice reading: "Man wanted for Robbery and Murder?"

He went in and applied for the job.

One night a police officer saw a Table Tennis Player looking for something under a street light. He asked him if he had lost something there.

The Table Tennis Player said: "I lost my keys in the alley."

"Why are you looking under the light," asked the police officer.

The Table Tennis Player responded: "It's a lot easier to look over
here."

The circus owner puts an ad in the newspaper for a part-time, trainee lion tamer.

A Table Tennis Player thinks it's an easy way to make some extra money, so he applies and gets the job.

"What do I do?," asks the Table Tennis Player.

"Simply hold the chair, the lion will obey," said the circus owner.

"And what should I do if the lion doesn't obey?," asked the Table Tennis Player.

"Crack the whip," said the circus owner."

"And if that doesn't work?," asked the Table Tennis Player.

"You have a revolver. Shoot it into the air," said the circus owner."

"And if that doesn't work, what do I do then?," asked the Table Tennis Player.

"Well then, throw shit at the lion," said the circus owner who was growing tired on this line of questioning."

"Where do I get that from?," asked the Table Tennis Player.

"Trust me on that," said the circus owner. "You'll have plenty!"

Have you heard about the Table Tennis Player who cheated Amtrak?

He bought a round-trip ticket to Washington and didn't go back.

An out-of-work Table Tennis Player was given the job of painting the lines down the middle of a highway. On his first day, he painted six miles; the next day three miles; the following day less than a mile.

The boss came up to him and said: "Your productivity is dropping rapidly. If you don't pick up your game, I'm going to have to let you go."

The Table Tennis Player replied: "I just can't do any better. Each day I keep getting farther away from the paint can."

What's the difference between a puppy and Table Tennis Player?

If you put a puppy in a room by itself for an hour, it'll eventually stop whining.

A man died and was taken to his place of eternal torment by the devil. As he passed sulfurous pits and shrieking sinners, he saw a man he recognized as his Table Tennis Player snuggling up to a beautiful woman.

"That's unfair!," he cried. "I have to roast for all eternity, and my Table Tennis Player gets to spend his afterlife with a beautiful woman."

"Shut up!," barked the devil, jabbing him with his pitchfork. "Who are you to question that woman's punishment?"

What's wrong with Table Tennis Player jokes?

Table Tennis Players don't think they're funny, and nobody else thinks they're jokes.

What is the difference between a catfish and a Table Tennis Player?

One is a scum sucking bottom dweller and the other is a fish.

Two Table Tennis Players went into a bar and ordered two drinks. They pulled out their lunch from their briefcases and started to eat.

The waiter became quite concerned and marched over and said: "You can't eat your own sandwiches in here!"

The Table Tennis Players looked at each other, shrugged their shoulders and then exchanged sandwiches.

Why is it good to have a Table Tennis Player as a passenger?

Because you can park in the handicapped zone.

"If there are any idiots in the room, will they please stand up," said the Table Tennis Player giving a lecture.

After a long silence, one attendee rose to his feet.

"Now," asked the Table Tennis Player. "Why do you consider yourself an idiot?"

"Well, actually I don't," replied the attendee. "But I hate seeing you standing up here all by yourself."

What do UFOs and smart Table Tennis Players have in common?

You hear about them all the time but you never see one.

How can you tell if a Table Tennis Player made the chocolate chip cookies?

There are M&Ms shells on the floor.

A successful Table Tennis Player parked his brand new Porsche in front of the office to show it off to his colleagues. As he got out, a truck came along too close to the curb and completely tore off the driver's side.

The Table Tennis Player immediately called 911 and in less than 5 minutes the law arrived. Before the police officer could ask any questions, the Table Tennis Player started screaming about how his brand-new car would never be the same again.

After the Table Tennis Player had finished his rant, the police officer shook his head in disbelief.

"I can't believe how materialistic you Table Tennis Players are," he said. "You're so focused on your possessions you don't notice anything else."

"How can you say that?," asked the Table Tennis Player.

The police officer replied: "Haven't you noticed that your left arm is missing from your elbow down? It was torn off when the truck hit you."

The Table Tennis Player looked down in absolute horror and screamed: "Where's my Rolex?"

Then there was a female Table Tennis Player who went swimming off the coast of Hawaii because she heard they were man-eating sharks.

Did you hear about the Table Tennis Player who wore a glove on one hand?

The forecaster said: "Tomorrow may be hot, but on the other hand, it could be cold."

A Table Tennis Player was on vacation and was told about a great restaurant in town, but thought it was closed because the sign in the window said: "Home Cooking."

A Table Tennis Player went into a bar with burnt feet. The barman said: "How did you burn your feet?"

The Table Tennis Player said: "Cooking spaghetti."

"How on earth can you burn your feet cooking spaghetti?," asked the astonished barman.

"Easy," said the Table Tennis Player. "I just followed the instructions. They said: Pierce top of can and stand in boiling water."

A Table Tennis Player went to a baseball game with a friend, but got stuck in traffic and arrived after the fifth inning. When they arrived, the score was still zero-zero.

"Oh good," said the Table Tennis Player, we haven't missed anything.

What do you call 16 Table Tennis Players standing in a room around a beer keg?

A dope ring.

Did you hear about the two not-so-bright Table Tennis Players who tried to make money selling watermelons?

They bought a truckload of melons for $5.00 each, and sold them for $5.00 each.

At the end of the day they sold everything they had bought, but couldn't work out why they had exactly the same amount of money as when they started.

"This isn't working," said one Table Tennis Player. "We're not making any money. What are we going to do?"

The other Table Tennis Player replied: "I guess we're going to have to get a bigger truck."

What's does a Table Tennis Player make for dinner?

Reservations.

A Table Tennis Player ordered a pizza. "Do you want it cut into four or eight slices?," asked the pizza maker.

The Table Tennis Player replied: "Better make it four, I'm not very
hungry."

A Table Tennis Player went to the doctor and asked how to have a better sex life. The doctor said: "Run five miles a day."

A week later the doctor called and said: "How is your sex life?"

The Table Tennis Player said: "I don't know, I'm 35 miles from home."

Did you hear about the Table Tennis Player who wore two jackets when he painted his house?

The instructions on the can said: "Put on two coats."

Why do Table Tennis Players laugh three times when they hear a joke?

Once when it is told, once when it is explained to them, and once when they understand it.

How do you make a Table Tennis Player's eyes light up?

Shine a flashlight in their ear.

Two Table Tennis Players rented a boat to go fishing in their local lake. Amazed at the number of fish they caught, they decided to come back the next day to try their luck again.

The first Table Tennis Player asked: "How will we find this spot again?"

The second Table Tennis Player takes a can of spray paint, paints an X on the bottom of the boat, and says: "We'll just look for this X tomorrow."

The first Table Tennis Player said: "You idiot! How do you know we'll get the same boat?"

Did you hear about the Buddhist Table Tennis Player who refused Novocaine during a root canal? The goal: transcend dental medication.

A priest was seated next to a Table Tennis Player on a flight to Texas. After the plane took off, the Table Tennis Player ordered a gin and tonic, which was brought and placed before him.

The flight attendant then asked the preacher if he wanted a drink.

Appalled, the preacher said: "I'd rather be tied up and taken advantage of by women of ill-repute, rather than let liquor touch my lips."

The Table Tennis Player then handed his drink back to the attendant and said: "Me too, I didn't know we had a choice."

How can you tell if a Table Tennis Player has been using the computer?

There's Wite-out on the screen.

Did you hear about the Table Tennis Player who turned up at a friend's house in a wet shirt?

The label said wash and wear.

During a visit to the doctor, a Table Tennis Player asks: "How do you determine whether a person should be put in an insane asylum?"

"The doctor said: "We fill up a bathtub and offer the person a teaspoon, cup and a bucket and ask them to empty the tub."

"I understand," said the Table Tennis Player. "A normal person would use the bucket because it's bigger than the spoon or the teacup."

"No," said the doctor. "A normal person would pull the plug. Do you want a bed near the window or the door?"

How can you be sure that Santa is a Table Tennis Player?

Every house has at least one door and window and Santa still chooses to come in through the chimney.

Did you hear about the Table Tennis Player who became a loan shark?

Lent out all his money and skipped town.

Why did the Table Tennis Player cut off all his fingers?

So he could write shorthand.

Two Table Tennis Players were adrift in a lifeboat. While rummaging
through the boat's provisions the first Table Tennis Player found a rusty old lamp.

He rubs the lamp and a genie suddenly appears. "Thank you for freeing me," said the genie. "Due to the current economic situation and the cutbacks, I can only grant you one wish.

"That's OK," replied the first Table Tennis Player. "All I want you to do is turn the entire ocean into beer."

The genie clapped his hands with a deafening crash, and suddenly the entire sea became beer.

The genie disappeared, and only the gentle lapping of beer on the hull broke the stillness as the two Table Tennis Players considered their circumstances.

"Nice going," said the second Table Tennis Player. "Now we're going to have to pee in the boat."

A Table Tennis Player checked into a room at his hotel and asked the lady at the registration desk if the porn channel in his room was disabled.

"No, it's regular porn, you sick bastard," replied the desk clerk.

The Personalized Edition

If you'd like to make this book your own, why not order a personalized copy for yourself or a friend. Simply go to www.dolyttle.com or www.thebesteverbook.com and enter your information. And we'll send you your very own copy of The Best Ever Book of YOUR NAME Jokes.

But the value doesn't end there. Not only will we put your name and picture on the cover and throughout the book, we'll also include one of your friends in the jokes so you can make fun of them.

At $19.95 per copy it's a great deal. If you're scared of the Internet, simply fill in the attached form and we'll do the rest.

ORDER! FORM

Dolyttle & Seamore
198 Garth Road Suite 2D
Scarsdale, NY 10583
212-496-8771 • info@dolyttle.com
(For faster service go to www.dolyttle.com)

Name _____

Address _____ Apt. _____

City _____ State _____ ZIP _____

Country _____

Email _____

Phone _____

Title: The Best Ever Book of _____ Jokes

Friend's Name _____

If you don't have a friend, don't worry about it. We'll nominate somebody be your friend, at absolutely no additional cost. Each book is $19.95 plus $3.99 shipping for the first book and $2.00 for each additional copy. Call for pricing for large orders and corporate prices.

WWW.DOLYTTLE.COM

Occupations

Account executive, Accountant, Acupuncturist, Actor, Administrative Assistant, Administrator, Aide, Air traffic controller, Ambulance officer, Analyst, Anesthesiologist, Announcer, Antique dealer, Architect, Assistant, Astronomer, Athlete, Audiologist, Auditor, Author, Baggage handler, Balloon artist, Banker, Baptist, Barber, Bartender, Beautician, Bee keeper, Benefit manager, Bill collector, Biologist, Bodybuilder, Book keeper, Boy scout, Breeder, Bricklayer, Builder, Building manager, Bus driver, Butcher, Camera operator, Camp counselor, Candy store owner, Car dealer, Caregiver, Carpenter, Carpet layer, Cartographer, Catholic, Chauffeur, Chef, Chemical engineer, Chemist, Chiropractor, Cinematographer, Civil engineer, Civil servant, Claim adjuster, Clerk, clown, Communist, Company director, Compliance officer, Computer engineer, Computer operator, Computer programmer, Conductor, Conference producer, Congressman, Conservationist, Cook, Copy editor, Courier, Criminal, Dancer, Data entry, Data entry clerk, Dealer, Debt collector, Deli owner, Delivery person, Democrat, Dental assistant, Dental hygienist, Dermatologist, Designer, Detailer, Detectives, Dispatcher, Doctor, Dog Walker, Doorman, Dressmaker, Drug dealer, Dry cleaner, Economist, Editor, Electrician, Emergency Medical Technician, Engineer, Engraver, Entertainer, Entrepreneur, Environmental engineer, Epidemiologist, Executive, Exporter, Farmer, Fencer, Fire fighter, Fisher man, Flight engineer, Food scientist, Food technologist, Fundraiser, Funeral director, Furniture maker, Garbage collector, Gardener, Geographer, Geologist, Girl scout, Golfer, Grave digger, Grocer, Guard, Guide, Hairdresser, Handyman, Hardware store owner, Hat maker, Hiring manager, Historian, Horticulturist, Host, Hostess, HR manager, Importer, Industrial engineer, Information system manager, Inspector, Instructor, Insurance agent, Interpreter, Janitor, Jew, Jeweler, Journalist, Judge, Laborer, Landscaper, Laundry assistant, Law clerk, Lawyer, Librarian, Life guard, Locksmith, Machinist, Magician, Mail sorter, Makeup artist, Manager, Managing director, Manicurist, Marketing manager, Marriage counselor, Mathematician, Meat slicer, Medical assistant, Messenger, Meter reader, Meteorologist, Midwife, Miner, Minister, Model, Motor cycle, Muslim, Naturopath, Norman, Nuclear engineer, Nurse, Nursing aide, Obstetrician, Occupational ther apist, Optician, Optometrist, Orthodontist, Paralegal, Parking inspector, Party planner, Pattern maker, Payroll clerk, Performer, Personnel manager, Pest control, Pharmacist, Pharmacy aide, Philosopher, Photographer, Physician, Physical ther apist, Physicist, Pilot, Pipe layer, Pizza parlor owner, Plumber, Podiatrist, Police officer, Political scientist, Politician, Porter, Postal worker, Postmaster, Potter, PR professional, President, Priest, Printer, Prison guard, Private detectives, Producer, Professor, Programmer, Projectionist, Proofreader, Psychiatric nurse, Psychologist, Purchasing manager, Rabbi, Radiographer, Real estate agent, Receptionist, Referee, Refrigeration mechanic, Registrar, Repairman, Reporter, Republican, Rigger, Roofer, Runner, Sailor, Sales manager, Sales rep, Salesperson, Scientist, Secretary, Security guard, Senator, Sher iff,

Shoe maker, Sign writer, Singer, Skier, Skin care specialist, Small business owner, Social worker, Socialist, Sociologist, Soldier, Sound technician, Speech ther apist, Spy, Statistician, Student, Superintendent, Supervisor, Surgeon, Surveillance officer, Surveyor, Swimmer, Swimming instructor, Tailor, Teaacher, Teaching assistant, Technician, Technologist, Technology writer, Telemarketer, Tennis player, Ther apist, Ticket collector, Title examiner, Tour guide, Travel agent, Truck driver, Tutor, Tire dealer, Umpire, Underwriter, Upholsterer, Urban planner, Urologist, Usher, Veterinarian, Waiter, Waitress, Web designer, Welder, Window washer, Woodworkers, Writer, Zookeeper, Zoologist..

Nationalities

Afghan, Albanian, Algerian, American, Andorran, Angolan, Anguillan, Antiguan, Barbadian, Argentine, Armenian, Australian, Austrian, Azerbaijani, Bahamian, Bahraini, Bangladeshi, Barbadian, Belarusian, Belgian, Belizean, Beninese, Bermudian, Bhutanese, Bolivian, Bosnian , Batswana, Brazilian, British, Bruneian, Bulgarian, Burkinabe, Burmese, Burundian, Cambodian, Cameroonian, Canadian, Cape Verdian, Caymanian, Central African, Chadian, Chilean, Chinese, Christmas Islander, Cocos Islander, Colombian, Comoran, Congolese, Costa Rican, Croat, Cuban, Cypriot, Czech, Dane, Djibouti, Dominica, Dutch, East Timorese, Ecuadorean, Egyptian, Emirati, Equatoguinean, Eritrean, Estonian, Ethiopian, Falkland Islander, Fijian, Filipino, Finnish, French, Gabonese, Gambian, Georgian, German, Ghanaian, Gibraltarian, Greek, Greenlander, Grenadian, Guadeloupian, Guatemalan, Guinean, Guinea-Bissauan, Guianese, Guyanese, Haitian, Herzegovinian, Honduran, Hungarian, Icelander, Indian, Indonesian, Iranian, Iraqi, Irish, Israeli, Italian, Jamaican, Japanese, Jordanian, Kazakhstani, Kenyan, Kiribati, Kittian, Kiwi, Korean, Kuwaiti, Kyrgyzstani, Laotian, Latvian, Lebanese, Liberian, Libyan, Liechtensteiner, Lithuanian, Luxembourger, Macedonian, Madagascan, Malagasy, Malawian, Malaysian, Maldivian, Malian, Maltese, Marshallese, Martinican, Mauritanian, Mauritian, Mahorais, Mexican, Micronesian, Moldovan, Monacan, Mongolian, Montserratian, Moroccan, Montenegrin, Mozambican, Myanmarese, Namibian, Nauruan, Nepalese, Netherlander, New Zealander, Nicaraguan, Niger, Nigerien, Nigerian, Norwegian, Omani, Pakistani, Palauan, Palestinian, Panamanian, Papua New Guinean, Paraguayan, Peruvian, Polish, Portuguese, Puerto Rican, Qatari, Reunionese, Romanian, Russian, Rwandan, Saint Helenian, Nevisian, Saint Lucian, Saint Vincentian, Salvadoran, Sammarinese, Sao Tomean, Saudi Arabian, Scottish, Senegalese, Serbian, Seychellois, Sierra Leonean, Singaporean, Slovak, Slovene, Solomon Islander, Somalian, Somali, South African, Spaniard, Sri Lankan, Sudan, Sudanese, Surinamer, Swazi, Swedish, Swiss, Syrian, Taiwanese, Tajik, Tanzanian, Thai, Tobagonian, Togolese, Tongan, Trinidadian, Tunisian, Turkish, Turkmen, Tuvaluan, Ugandan, Ukrainian, Uruguayan, Uzbekistani, Vanuatu, Venezuelan, Vietnamese, Virgin Islander, Welsh, Yemeni, Zambian, Zimbabwean.

Sports

Adventure, Archery, Athletics, Badminton, Baseball, Basketball, Bowling, Boxing, Canoe, Cricket, Cycling, Diving, Equestrian, Fencing, Football, Golf, Gymnastics, Handball, Hockey, Jockey, Kayak, Martial Arts, , Mountaineering, Netball, Orienteering, Ping Pong, Polo, Racing, Rowing, Rugby, Sailing, Shooting, Soccer, Softball, Surfing, Swimming, Table Tennis, Volleyball, Weightlifting, Wresting.

Religion

Atheist, Buddhist, Christian, Catholic, Protestant, Unitarian, Baptist, Jewish, Confucianist, Hare Krishna, Hindi, Muslim, Jehovah's Witness, Mormon, Rastafarian, Scientologist, Seventh-day Adventist, Sikh, Pagan, Witch.

Political Parties

Communist, Conservative, Democrat, Independent, Labour, Liberal, Libertarian, Non-Voter, Republican, Socialist, Tea Party.

Or

Write Your own

THE BEST EVER GUIDE TO _____ JOKES

Lots and Lots of Jokes Specially Repurposed for _____

VISIT WWW.DOLYTTLE.COM TO FIND OUT MORE.